YOU'RE COOKIN' TONIGHT

the quickest way to the bedroom
is through the kitchen

ANDY MORANTZ

ISBN: 1-4392-3814-6
ISBN-13: 9781439238141

Visit www.booksurge.com to order additional copies.

CONTENTS

FOREWORD

Now that I've caught your attention with the title, let me explain. While I'm not promising a guaranteed path to carnal bliss, if you follow the advice and recipes here you will have a much better shot at it.

Keep in mind the recipes in this book are just everyday food – Nothing super fancy or "romantic." The romance isn't in the food. It's in the **LABOR.** Here is my best piece of advice: Don't just plan and cook dinner occasionally...like Mother's Day or your anniversary (when you remember it.) That doesn't cut it. **You must plan, shop, cook and CLEAN-UP on a regular basis.** If you do, you will get away with a multitude of sins...and maybe even invent a few new ones.

Too many men don't know how easy cooking a good meal can be. After all, you know what they say – "If you can read, you can cook," so the mere fact that you are reading this book bodes well for your culinary future. I will show you some tips, some mistakes to avoid, and if you're really adventuresome, how to throw a dinner party where nobody throws up.

Trust me on this, being a good cook will work wonders for your "relationship." Who knows, you might even like it. For sure you'll enjoy the perks.

HINTS ON CLEAN-UP

As mom says, "Cleaning is important." Remember, you're not selling your food here as much as your LABOR. As in "Labor of Love." You're showing your spouse how much you love her by not making her clean all the time. Sometimes she can pitch in, but don't expect to get lucky on those nights.

The biggest time saver in the kitchen clean-up department is CLEAN AS YOU GO. When you're done with a pot, wash it out. If you need another pot for something, use the same one and clean it again. Clean your counter tops and cutting boards after each phase of preparation. Wash off your utensils and knives between jobs and use them again. By the end of the meal, all you'll have left to do is pack up the leftovers to rot in the fridge and load the dishwasher. No dishwasher? No problem. If all the prep dishes are already clean, all you have to do is swab down the plates (don't forget to soap them, duh) and put them in the drying rack.

For obvious environmental reasons, I don't recommend using paper or plastic plates and throwing them away after dinner. That's just PLAIN LAZY cowboy.

To avoid stuck on muck on your baking dishes, line them with foil. (I have a confession to make. I've been known to get so frustrated trying to pry the nasty bits off the bottom of a pan used for roasting chicken, that I've actually thrown it away when no one was looking. I never said I was perfect.)

THE GEAR

To fully accomplish your mission in the kitchen, you'll need the proper gear. Half of the junk currently cluttering up your kitchen is useless and can be sold as scrap. For instance, you do not need a giant food processor. Sure, they work great, but in our system they create TOO MANY THINGS TO WASH. Nobody cares if your cukes (an inside word for cucumber) are perfectly sliced. Your wife will be amazed you knew they weren't raw pickles. You can get a smaller one that attaches to an immersion blender.

So if you have more in your kitchen than is listed here, get up, put it all in a box and get it out of "your" kitchen. Clutter is the enemy. You need space to work. And you need a radio.

Here is a list of necessary gear for cooking:

1. **A sharp knife of the expensive variety.** A ten-inch Wustoff Trident chef's knife is a good bet and no, they aren't paying me to say that. You will not be sorry, even if you pay upwards of one hundred dollars for a good one. Don't buy a macho-sized jungle tool. You aren't butchering cows here. Ask the guy in that knife shop in the mall that you never go into for advice. Tell him you'll be chopping veggies and slicing raw meat and chicken, and he'll take it from there. DON'T BUY YOUR KNIFE IN THE SUPERMARKET. It will be your friend and most important tool, so choose one with love. Remember you'll be hacking screaming tomatoes with it, so it needs to be sharp, true and comfortable ... like an old easy chair (but don't sit on it.)

2. **A set of wooden spoons and spatulas.** *These* you can buy in the supermarket. They are essential for eggs and stir fries. Anything you throw in a pan needs to be moved around with a spoon of some variety, and you don't want to mess up your pots and pans with metal. Don't worry if they break. They're cheap. Just get the pieces out of the chili first.

3. **A potato masher**. This is not a wimpy cop-out. It makes better mashed potatoes than a fork, like Mom used to use. She was wrong. Stop crying. It's no surprise. Get a hold of yourself.

4. **Measuring spoons.** I like the cheap ones that are all connected together like a baby rattle. Takes me back....

5. **Wire whisk.** A cheap metal one is fine. Don't let the chatty guy at the cooking store sell you a fancy-schmancy one with a graphite handle or some such golf-like accessory.

6. **An immersion blender.** You will need one of these to fix lumpy sauces or gravies and make soups smooth. Believe me, you can royally screw up a sauce or gravy and save it by pulverizing it with an immersion blender. Most immersion blenders have a small food processor attachment to make things that need to be super whizzed up like pesto, etc. And when you use an immersion blender your friends will think you deserve your own cooking show.

7. **Measuring cups.** Get a set for dry ingredients, as well as 2 and 8-cup Pyrex-style measuring cups for wet stuff.

8. **Stainless-steel Asian wok**. Not an electric Teflon wok. Not an aluminum wok. A *stainless steel Asian wok*. You will be using the wok to impress your wife and friends into thinking that you are a hip gourmand. Besides, food tastes better in a well-seasoned stainless steel wok. You can get them for cheap at any Asian market or cooking supply store.

9. **Any kind of can opener**. It doesn't matter what kind as long as it works. (You won't be opening that many cans anyway. You will notice there aren't a lot of canned ingredients in the recipes in this book. You will be making most meals from scratch; some use ingredients that aren't normally even made by home cooks, like Hoisin sauce or BBQ sauce.)

10. **A wine/bottle opener**. For wine…and beer. A chef's best friend.

11. **Cheese grater.** You will not, repeat after me, *will not* used sliced, processed cheese in any way, shape or form. And good cheese is best grated if melting is desired.

12. A set of good **stainless steel sauce pans** with lids and a steamer insert.

13. **A ten-inch iron skillet**. You can steal one from your mom like I did. She's using her Teflon wok and will never miss it.

14. **Cookie sheets**. Steal these from your mom too. She hasn't baked since you left her house anyway.

15. **Casserole dish with cover**.

16. **Foil and plastic wrap**. You will be lining dishes with foil to save washing baked- on food. You'll use the plastic to wrap leftovers. Don't throw them away. They are fun to watch turn into plants in the fridge.

17. **Bowls**. Large ones. Small ones. Plastic, glass, even paper ones (if you tend to be wasteful as well as lazy like some of us...but shame on you.) Stack them carefully or you'll have bowl movement every time you open the cabinet.

18. **Baking dishes** (13 x 9 and/or 8 x 8)

19. **Strainer**

20. **Cutting boards.** You'll need two large resin boards: one for veggies, one for protein, and never the twain shall meet.

SPICES AND CONDIMENTS

Kosher Salt*
Peppercorns* (pepper grinder)
Allspice
Basil
Chili Powder
Cumin
Garlic Powder
Onion Powder
Oregano
Rosemary
Sweet Paprika
Thyme

BBQ Sauce (anything from KC is best, but I'm biased)
Chili Sauce
Hoisin Sauce
Hot Salsa
Mild Salsa
Molasses
Mustard (Dijon)
Soy Sauce
Steak Sauce
Toasted Sesame Oil
Worcestershire Sauce

Henceforth referred to as S and P. S and P is what all the high end chefs call salt and pepper. Who knew?

A WORD ABOUT KNIFE SKILLS

I think that cooking is the only time when you can use the words "knife" and "skill" in the same sentence. If your 7-year-old uses it at school it's sayonara second grade.

("Hey Billy, guess what? I've been watching my dad and now I have righteous knife skills.")

The most important thing to learn about knife skills is DON'T CUT YOURSELF.

That means take it slow. Use a sharp knife. I know this sounds like a contradiction, but a sharp knife needs less force, therefore there's less chance of it slipping. I would be lying to you if I told you I never cut myself. I have what I call "stupid" cuts on my hands. Stupid as in trying to go too fast or looking up to talk to my imaginary friends while using a sharp knife on a frozen bagel. The other way to get a "stupid" cut is chop things like your mom did using the knife against her thumb instead of a cutting board. Who invented that technique? It must have been an insecure four-fingered man who wanted everyone else to look like he did. So, unless someone is going to come into your kitchen and measure your dice, just be careful and you'll be fine.

A WORD ABOUT VEGGIES

Fresh.

OK, sorry for being cheeky. Seriously though, there are some good guidelines for picking fresh veggies. If I miss one here it's cuz I didn't gradiate from cookin' school and admittedly I don't know everything. Don't tell my wife.

BELL PEPPERS (RED, YELLOW, GREEN, EVEN PURPLE! WHO WOULDA THUNK?)
The pepper should be vibrantly colored, and firm to the touch. Look out for little wrinkles that are starting to form on the pepper.

BROCCOLI
It should be deep green in color and firm to the touch. Limp broccoli is not good to eat.

CARROTS
Can you bend the carrot? Then put it back. It should be very crisp and firm. Don't bend too hard or it might break. You break it you buy it.

CAULIFLOWER

Cauliflower is usually firm to the touch so that technique won't work here. But look for little brown spots forming between the brain-like bumps. That signals an old cauli. And it needs enough help as it is to taste good, so get a fresh one.

EGGPLANT

You won't find an eggplant recipe in this book. I hate eggplant. But I think a good one is bright purple and firm but not rock-solid to the touch. Again, if it's ginormous it's probably going to be pulpy. Blech.

GARLIC

I buy fresh garlic, not the kind in the jar. Don't be tempted by convenience. The prepared garlic is stronger in flavor and the recipes here all call for fresh garlic. If you do use prepared garlic, cut down on the amount or the food will be mega garlic-ized.

Garlic Tip: Mincing garlic is easy. And if anyone sees you doing it the way I show you here, they will know you are a cooking force to be reckoned with. Lay the garlic on cutting board and smash it with the flat side of your knife. Take off the skin. Chop the smashed garlic. Done. (Remember to wash your hands afterwards or your wife will think you're trying to scare off vampires.)

MUSHROOMS

There are many varieties of mushrooms, almost as many as beer. For the purposes of this book we deal with two kinds: **white button mushrooms** (the kind that come pre-packaged) and large **portobello mushrooms** (sometimes packaged, sometimes in a bulk bin.)

With button mushrooms, look for the stem of the mushroom to be attached to the top all the way around. If you can see the little "gills" on the underside of the mushroom, it is past its prime and will be rubbery.

Portobello mushrooms, when packaged, are harder to check but are usually fine...although slightly more expensive. Bulk portobellos should be thick, meaty and firm to the touch. You'll be able to see their "gills," but that's OK.

Mushroom Tip: There is a debate in the "food community" about washing mushrooms. Some say that rinsing makes them waterlogged and advise simply rubbing them off with a cloth or paper towel. I've tried that method so will weigh in on the subject. Even if the mushroom takes on a tiny bit of water, it's still better than missing a big hunk of mud when you're cooking them. Nothing says ick like a dish made with mud. So I wash my mushrooms, drain them and dry them off. Just one man's opinion.

ONIONS
Make sure they're not at all gooey or soggy. That is the sign of a **rotten onion**. You'd be surprised to actually see them in the store, but you will.

'TATERS (BAKING, RED, YUKON, SWEET)
Look for potatoes with as few brown rotten spots as possible. Rotten is bad. Squeeze each one and make sure it's very firm to the touch. Also, don't buy potatoes that have a lot of green visible under the skin. Because potatoes are from the (poisonous) nightshade family, the green denotes toxins. I've never gotten sick from eating

them, but why take chances especially when "getting lucky with the lady" is in the balance. If all the store has are potatoes with green showing, peel them very well to remove.

TOMATOES

In my neck of the woods (the upper Midwest), many tomatoes are only good during late spring and summer. A good tomato is soft but not too soft (unless you want it for your neighbor's cat) and bright red in color. Vine-ripe tomatoes are usually a good bet, but expensive. Roma tomatoes are good almost all year round.

But now that we're on the subject of tomatoes I'm going to air one of my food pet peeves. Why do restaurants insist on serving under-ripe tomatoes on their salads? They taste like wood and it's an insult to the palate. If a tomato isn't ripe DON'T SERVE IT. Whew, I feel better, thanks.

ZUCCHINI

It should be firm to the touch. If you can bend it in half, leave it. Also, size matters. Super-huge zuchs are pulpy and woody tasting. Yuck. The "average" decent zucchini is about 6-inches long. Yum.

THE RECIPES

Although some of these recipes may seem simple and obvious, it will be helpful to have them all in one place. I'd like it if this was the only cookbook you ever needed. And that you used it so often, you'd have to keep buying new copies.

(Prep time and serving sizes will be given when appropriate. Prep time indicates the time in which it takes you to prepare the ingredients for cooking.)

(On the "covered/uncovered" issue…. I hate it when a recipe does not indicate this. Leaving this small tidbit of information out can ruin a meal. You have my word, I will ALWAYS tell you when to cover and uncover. Just like I tell my wife….)

THE GREEN FOOD GROUP:
VEGETABLES

MIXED VEGGIES "CHINESE" STYLE
Prep Time: 10 minutes
Serves 2 to 4

Ingredients:
- 2 tablespoons peanut, olive or canola oil
- ½ onion, sliced thin
- 1 clove of garlic, chopped
- ½ red or green bell pepper, sliced thin
- ½ head cabbage, sliced thin
- 8 oz. button mushrooms, sliced
- 1/3 cup soy sauce
- ½ teaspoon red chili flakes (optional)
- 1 teaspoon toasted sesame oil

Heat oil in wok or skillet until SCREAMING hot, but not burning. Add the onion and garlic and cook for 30 seconds or so. Add the rest of the veggies and continue cooking on high for 2 minutes, moving constantly around in the pan. Add soy sauce and red pepper flakes. It's an impressive sound when the soy sauce hits the pan, so make sure someone is paying attention.   Turn off heat. Add toasted sesame oil.

STEAMED VEGGIES

Much of cooking is a process rather than a recipe. Steaming veggies is a process. You can use any vegetable you like. Some vegetables are more suitable for steaming than others. Broccoli, cauliflower, carrots, asparagus and cabbage all work well; mushrooms, zucchini, and peppers do not. They get slimy and gross, and most people don't like slimy food. (Although I've heard raw oysters are very popular, I personally don't see the allure of letting a raw sea creature slither down my throat.)

Anyway, here's how to steam veggies:
You'll need your steamer. Add 2-inches of water to your sauce pan, then insert steamer into the pan. Add veggies to the insert. Cover. Bring to boil over high heat. Lower heat to a bare simmer and steam for 10 to 15 minutes depending on the veggie. It's OK to check after a few minutes by lifting the lid. (Warning, don't park your mug over the pan or you'll get a nice burn. That is not impressive to your diners.)

When the veggies look bright in color and are soft but not mushy when you fork 'em, they're done. Remove from steamer, dump in a bowl with some melted butter, salt and pepper. If you're using the veggies in other recipes, some chefs give instructions for "shocking" them in a bowl of ice water to retain their color. This makes for great TV but in reality it uses up all of your available ice that you need to make cocktails, and it gives you another bowl to clean up. (Remember our mantra: Try to make as few dirty dishes as possible. Even though it may seem fair that the cook shouldn't have to do the clean up, it doesn't work that way. Remember, you're on a mission to booty, and failing to clean up your own kitchen gains you points in the "leave me the heck alone" column.)

SALAD (IF YOU'RE LAZY)

Ingredients:
- prewashed romaine lettuce hearts
- your favorite bottled dressing

Tear lettuce into bowl. Add dressing. Toss. Eat. What? You want a fancy salad recipe? OK, fine. Keep reading.

FANCY SALAD (IF YOU'RE NOT)
Prep Time: 15 minutes
Serves 2 to 4

Honey Mustard Vinaigrette:

Ingredients:
- 3 tablespoons of your favorite vinegar...(except the nasty cider vinegar that some people use to wash windows. I've always wondered why someone would wash their windows with something that smelled so terrible. Kind of defeats the purpose of having an inviting home, doesn't it?)
- 1 tablespoon Dijon mustard
- ¼ cup olive oil
- 1 tablespoon honey
- S and P

In a small mixing bowl, whisk the vinegar and the mustard until smooth. Drizzle in the oil, whisking the whole time. Add the honey, a pinch of S and a couple/three grinds of P. (Wow that sounds weird.) So the dressing is done, what's next? Here are some other ingredients you can add to your fancy salad. Besides the lettuce try these options:

- ½ apple, cored and chopped
- ½ cup grated cheddar cheese
- 1 stalk celery, chopped
- 1 small carrot, chopped
- ½ cup walnuts, pecans or cashews (raw, roasted, salted, unsalted it doesn't matter...don't over think. It's just a salad)
- You want more ideas, try:
- garbanzo beans
- tomato (only if they're ripe...refer to "How to How to Pick Veggies")
- cucumbers

Toss all ingredients in large bowl with the lettuce. Add dressing and toss.

ASIAN COLE SLAW
Prep Time: 5 minutes
Serves 2 to 4

Ingredients:
- ½ cup peanut oil
- 1/3 cup rice wine vinegar
- 1 tablespoon soy sauce
- 1 teaspoon toasted sesame oil
- ½ teaspoon pepper flakes
- ½ teaspoon sugar
- One bag of cole slaw mix (I don't favor using a lot of prepared ingredients but the slaw mix is great because you don't have a giant food processor, right? And that's the only way you can really prep the cabbage and carrots for this recipe.)

Whisk the oil and rice wine vinegar in large bowl until well combined. Add the rest of the ingredients, except the slaw, and combine. Add the entire bag of slaw mix and let this marinate for 30 minutes or so before serving. Give another toss to combine.

VEGGIES SAUTÉED IN WHITE WINE
Prep Time: 15 minutes
Serves 2 to 4

Ingredients:
- 2 tablespoons of olive oil
- 8 oz. button mushrooms, sliced
- ½ onion, sliced
- 1 zucchini, sliced
- 1/2 cup white wine (Chefs and cookbook writers always say never cook with a wine you wouldn't drink. But I know you. You'd DRINK just about any wine. I'm going to suggest you use a DRY white wine)
- S and P
- 2 tablespoons of chopped fresh herbs like parsley, basil or thyme (optional)

Heat oil in skillet over high heat. Add the veggies and cook for 2 to 3 minutes, until the onion starts to look clear. Add the wine, S and P to taste and let cook for another 2 minutes, until the alcohol smell cooks out. Depending on how much of the wine you've been drinking, you may not be able to tell, but 2 minutes should do it. Add the fresh herbs and serve.

ROASTED VEGGIES
PrepTime: 15 Minutes
Serves 2 to 4

Much like steaming vegetables, roasting them is more of a process than a recipe. But the following recipe is good because it can be served hot, cold or at room temperature.

Ingredients:
- 3 portobello mushrooms, sliced
- 1 red onion, sliced
- 2 zucchini, cut long-ways into thick slices
- 1 red bell pepper, cut in rings
- ½ cup olive oil
- 3 cloves of garlic, chopped
- juice of 1 lemon
- A few sprigs of fresh thyme or rosemary
- S and P to taste

Heat oven to 400° F. In a large bowl, thoroughly combine all ingredients. Pour onto a large baking sheet. Roast in the oven 30 to 40 minutes until veggies look shiny, soft and a little brown around the edges, but not burnt.

ROASTED CAULIFLOWER
Prep Time: 10 minutes
Serves 2 to 4

You may not be a big cauliflower fan, but my wife likes this recipe so here it is. (Points, guys. It's all about the points.) Besides, roasted cauliflower is much sweeter than steamed or boiled ... and everything tastes good with enough butter.

Ingredients:
- ½ head of cauliflower hacked into pieces the size of a strawberry. (You can go through the trouble of separating the florets neatly, but that's time consuming and it tastes the same. All that stuff they say about tasting with your eyes – it's all fine and good if you have the patience. Which often I don't.)
- 2 tablespoons of butter, cubed
- S and P to taste

Heat oven to 400° F. Put the cauliflower in a small baking dish. Dot with the butter, season with S and P. Put in the oven, UNCOVERED, for 15 to 20 minutes. When done, florets should be pale beige in color. Toss around in the butter and serve.

BRAISED BRUSSELS SPROUTS
Prep Time: 10 Minutes
Serves 2 to 4

I know I'm stepping out on a limb here with two unpopular vegetables in a row, but trust me, this is a good way to cook Brussels sprouts.

Ingredients:
- 1 tablespoon olive oil
- 8 to 10 Brussels sprouts cut in half (Remove the tough outer layer and cut off the stem while you're at it)
- ½ cup chicken stock
- ¼ cup soy sauce
- P to taste

Heat olive oil over medium heat in skillet. Add the Brussels sprouts cut-side down in a single layer. Cook for a couple of minutes until they start to brown. Grind on some pepper. Add the chicken stock and soy sauce. . Cover and simmer 10 minutes.

SAUTÉED SPINACH
Prep Time: 10 minutes
Serves 2 to 4

Ingredients:
- 2 tablespoons olive oil
- 2 cloves of chopped garlic
- 1 shallot, chopped (If you've never used a shallot before, they're a cross between an onion and garlic. In the store, they're usually found with the onions and the garlic)
- one bag of pre-washed spinach
- pinch of nutmeg
- S and P

Heat oil in a large skillet over medium-high heat. Add the shallots and the garlic and cook for a minute or so, but don't burn. (Overcooked garlic is nasty. Save nasty for later.) Add the spinach all at once and watch the fun! What starts out as a bowling ball size of greens quickly shrinks down to almost nothing in the pan. (Kind of like jumping into a cold swimming pool, if you get my drift.) Add a pinch of nutmeg and S and P to taste. The spinach is ready to serve as soon as it wilts. Serve with a slotted spoon to ditch some of the cooking liquid.

CREAMED SPINACH
Prep Time: 10 minutes
Serves 2 to 4

If you serve this dish with a baked potato and a steak, your dinner guests will think you have channeled the chef at a top end steakhouse. Unless, of course, you ruin their steaks....which is highly unlikely because you're a guy, and guys are born with the innate ability to slap their meat onto a bed of hot coals.

Ingredients:
- Sautéed spinach from above recipe (**remove the spinach from the pan with a slotted spoon to get rid of the extra moisture or you'll have creamed spinach soup)**
- 1/4 cup heavy cream
- ½ cup freshly grated Parmesan cheese

Heat oven to 350° F. Put spinach in small baking dish and pour heavy cream over. Top with the Parmesan cheese. Bake about 20 minutes, or until bubbly.

CORN ON THE COBB
Prep Time: 5 minutes
1 ear serves one

Ingredients:
- 1 ear of corn per person
- splash of milk
- ½ teaspoon of sugar
- 1 tablespoon of butter per ear of corn (at least)
- S and P

Put the corn in a pot and add enough water to cover the corn by one-inch. Add a splash of milk and the sugar. Bring to a boil. Turn off the heat and cover tightly. Let the corn sit for 20 minutes. Remove the corn to a platter and serve with butter and S and P.

THE WHITE FOOD GROUP
(STARCHES AND OTHER SIDES)

By now you know this is my clever grouping system for dishes. They aren't all going to be white, but I think you're savvy enough to figure that out.

BAKED POTATO
Prep Time: 1 minute
1 potato serves one

Ingredients:
- 1 1-lb. russet potato per person
- desired toppings

Heat oven to 450 °F. Wash potato and jab skin with a fork a couple of times. Place directly on the oven rack and bake for 1 hour.

I know this sounds simple, but there are some mistakes that people make that can mess up a potato, like wrapping it in foil. They do that at low-end steak houses to keep them fresh. And guess what? They're never fresh, are they? They're cold, clumpy and gluey inside.

If you MUST hold a baked potato at temperature after cooking, just wrap it in a clean kitchen towel and keep it on the counter. It will stay hot for a pretty long time.

Another mistake people make is too low of an oven temperature. Anything less than 450° F. and you're steaming the potato, which takes forever and you end up with a gluey potato. Just like slimy food, people don't really like gluey food either.

Here's a tip. Whenever you're making baked potatoes for dinner, double the recipe and put the leftover 'taters' in the fridge for use in the next recipe.

Microwave tip: Cook the potatoes (up to 4 at a time) in the microwave on high for 5 minutes then put them into the hot oven for 30 minutes.

HOME FRIES
Prep Time: 5 minutes
1 potato serves 2 people

Ingredients:
- leftover baked potatoes
- 3 tablespoons of oil
- S and P

Slice the potatoes in ½-inch rounds. Heat the oil in a skillet until hot but not smoking. Add the potatoes in a single layer. Fry on one side until golden brown, then turn and fry the other side.

Drain on baking rack (If you don't want to clean the rack, nobody will turn you in to the food police for draining them on paper towels.) Season with S and P while they're hot.

MASHED POTATOES
Prep Time: 5 minutes
2 to 3 potatoes person

If mashed potatoes remind you of dorm food, never fear. This simple recipe will have the hash sloppers worshipping your masher.

Ingredients:
- 2 to 3 red potatoes per person
- butter
- milk or heavy cream
- S and P

Boil potatoes in enough salted water to cover by at least 1-inch for 30 to 40 minutes over high heat, uncovered. Stick a fork in one. It's done when the fork comes out easily. Drain taters and return to pan. Hit the pan with some more heat to evaporate the remaining water in the pan.. Don't walk away from them at this stage. It only takes 30 seconds to go from removing the extra water to burning them onto the bottom of the pan.

Add 2 to 3 tablespoons of butter and enough milk or cream to moisten. It's best if the milk or cream is heated, but if you don't want to wash another pan they'll still be good. Grab your trusty potato masher out of its shrine and prepare to pulverize the little guys right in the pan.

SMASH SMASH STIR STIR SMASH SMASH STIR STIR

Put into a serving bowl, or if you're trailer parkin' it, serve them right from the pan. This however, leads to a whole different romantic experience.

Hint: Do not use an electrical whipping type of appliance for this job. In my opinion (and again, this is my book which means that at least for the time being, I'm right) it makes them pasty, sticky, gluey and gross.

CARAMELIZED SWEET POTATOES WITH PECANS
Prep Time: 5 minutes
1 potato per person

Some people don't like sweet potatoes. And some other people try to convince other people to like sweet potatoes by making them into a casserole that hides behind little baby marshmallows. (Where do they get little baby marshmallows anyway? Probably the same place they get Game Hens.) This recipe won't flip a sweet tater-hater. But it's mighty swell anyway.

Ingredients:
- one sweet potato per person (yams work, too)
- brown sugar
- pecans (halves or pieces, whichever is cheaper at the market)
- butter
- nutmeg
- S and P

Peel and cut sweet potatoes into 1-inch cubes. Boil for 5 minutes. Drain. Put sweet potatoes into buttered baking dish. Sprinkle the top with a light coating of brown sugar and a handful of pecans to taste. Dot with butter. Add a dash of nutmeg, salt and pepper to taste. Put in a heated 350° F. oven, UNCOVERED, for 45 minutes. Halfway through the cooking time, remove and toss the Ingredients in the baking dish to coat and return to the oven for the remainder of the cooking time. They'll be soft and nicely coated when they're done. Add more butter if you want.

BAKED BEANS
Prep Time: 5 Minutes
Serves 6 to 8

This is one of the few recipes in this book that calls for almost all prepared Ingredients. (You could soak raw beans over night, cook them up and put them in this recipe, but that's WAY too much work.) What makes these beans really pop is adding plenty of leftover BBQ meat. Whenever you make pork chops or steaks on the grill, freeze the leftovers so you have them for this bean recipe. I'm a Kansas City boy and it's how all the best KC BBQ joints do it. Who am I to argue with Kansas City BBQ? It's the best in the country, after all!

Ingredients:
- one large can of vegetarian baked beans (I use vegetarian because I don't like the little squishy piece of fat back bacon they toss in there to make them look authentic.)
- 1 cup of leftover meat from the grill (You should have a supply hogging freezer space)
- ½ cup of your favorite BBQ Sauce
- ¼ cup of packed brown sugar
- 1 tablespoon of Dijon Mustard
- 1 tablespoon of soy sauce
- 1 tablespoon of Worcestershire Sauce

Put the beans in a colander and drain off some of the canned tomato sauce. Dump them in a bowl and mix in all the other Ingredients. Put the beans in a casserole dish and bake, COVERED, in a 300° F. oven for 1 hour. UNCOVER and bake another ½ hour, until bubbly. If you have the time, cook them in a 225° F. oven for 3 hours, COVERED.

SIMPLE PASTA DRESSED TO IMPRESS
Prep Time: 5 Minutes
Serves 2 to 4

Ingredients:
- 1 lb. package of the pasta of your choice (anything will work)
- 2 tablespoons olive oil
- 2 tablespoons butter ... (or more, to taste)
- 2 cloves of mashed garlic or more if you're a garlic freak. (This is when I prefer to use a garlic press rather than the smash and chop method. I don't want any little pieces of garlic in this dish. If you don't have a garlic press, after you chop the garlic, mash it with your knife mixed with a little salt on your cutting board)
- ½ cup grated Parmesan cheese
- S and P to taste

Prepare the pasta according to the packaged instructions. Drain. In a large skillet, melt the butter and olive oil over low heat and add the garlic, Parmesan cheese, salt and pepper. Add the drained pasta to the pan along with the cheese, mix and serve.

RICE

Cook rice according to the package instructions. You can use a prepared chicken stock instead of water for more flavor. And if you mess it up, don't come crying to me. I've been cooking my entire adult life and I've been known to totally destroy a pot of rice.

SOUTHWESTERN CORN PUDDING
Prep Time: 5 Minutes
Serves 4 to 6

I know I keep talking about not using pre-packaged Ingredients, but this is one I made up to be a super fast and easy side dish. People like it, so I continue to make it.

Ingredients:
- 1 small box of corn bread mix
- 1 small can of mild or hot diced green chilies, depending on your taste
- 1 can creamed corn
- 2 cups shredded cheese (reserve ½ cup for topping)
- 3 tablespoons of melted butter
- 1 egg

Mix all Ingredients in a bowl. Pour into a buttered casserole dish, top with remaining ½ cup cheese and bake at 350° F. for 45 minutes.

BAKED MAC AND CHEESE
Prep Time: 15 minutes
Serves 4 to 6

There are basically three ways to make mac and cheese. One is to use the boxed kind with the powdered cheese (not really fit for human consumption, that's why your kids love it.)

The next is the "boil the noodles and dump in a bunch of processed cheese" kind. (Which is how you learned to make it in college and that didn't help you much in the S-E-X department, did it?)

And then there's Baked Mac and Cheese. Made properly, this is one of the most sublime comfort foods on the planet – a miracle of Comfort Food Science.

Ingredients:
- 1 lb. box of elbow macaroni
- 2 cups white sauce (see recipe on page 48)
- 4 cups grated sharp cheddar cheese
- ½ cup of Panko bread crumbs
- 1/4 cup melted butter

Cook macaroni according to package instructions. Drain and put back in its cooking vessel. Prepare the white sauce according to the recipe on page 48. Add the cheese to the warm white sauce and stir until melted. Add the cheese sauce to the macaroni and pour into a baking dish. Combine the bread crumbs and the melted butter. It should have the consistency of wet sand. Cover the top of the mac and cheese with the bread crumbs and bake, UNCOVERED, at 350° F. for 30 to 45 minutes, until the bread crumbs are brown and the cheese is bubbly. After you pull it out of the oven, let it sit for 15 minutes before serving to let it set up.

If you're feeling "craytive" as they say here in the Midwest...you can add some cooked chopped bacon, leftover chicken, or chopped tomatoes to the dish before you put it into the baking dish.

THE BROWN FOOD GROUP:
PROTEINS

(THIS INCLUDES ALL PROTEINS, BROWN OR OTHERWISE.)

BEEF

STEAK ANDREW ELLIS
Prep Time: 15 minutes
Serves 2 to 4

- sirloin tip round steak (Buying the meat: Tell your butcher you need sirloin tip round steak sliced thin, allow 6 oz. per person)
- ½ cup white wine
- ¼ cup olive oil
- 1 clove garlic, minced
- S and P
- 2 tablespoons butter
- 8 oz. button mushrooms, cut into thirds
- ½ onion, chopped

Combine wine, oil, garlic, salt and pepper to taste in shallow pan to cover meat. Let meat marinate at least 1 hour in the fridge.

Heat butter in skillet over medium-high heat. When butter is bubbly, add meat. Remember, this is a thin cut

THE BROWN FOOD GROUP

and it's been marinating (partially cooking because of the acid in the wine.) It will only need to cook a couple of minutes per side for medium- rare. Add the mushrooms, onions, and ½ the marinade when turning meat. Cover and cook for a couple more minutes until the onions are soft.

HAMBURGERS
Prep Time: 5 minutes
Serves 2

Allow 6 oz. hamburger per burger for a nice-sized portion. There is no such thing as a measly "Quarter Pounder" in *your* house!

A note on meat: The best burgers have some fat. If you use super lean (93%), the end product will be dry. I use 85% lean. You can get 75% lean, but don't... your heart will thank you.

Put meat in mixing bowl. Add 3 dashes of Worcestershire Sauce and a pinch of salt and pepper. Mix gently together and form into 2 patties. Cook in preheated skillet on medium heat; 3 to 4 minutes for rare, 4 to 5 for medium, 5 to7 for well. Drain on paper towels.

Note: On BBQ Grill the same cooking times apply. Watch for flare-up that might cause your burgers to burn.

MEAT LOAF
Prep Time: 10 minutes
Serves 6 to 8

Most meat loaf recipes use a combination of beef, pork and veal. I use ground turkey to take the place of the pork and veal. It's cheaper than veal and has less fat. This is a case where using lean ground meats is OK because we're adding a bunch of other stuff to keep it from drying out. Besides, we all grew up with dry meatloaf, why change now? Just kidding…this recipe is a good one, and by that I mean "it makes great sandwiches the next day."

I don't like the texture of bits and pieces of cooked veggies in my meatloaf, so none are called for here. But you're the cook, so you can add whatever you want to your meatloaf. I had a friend who used to hide a hot dog and a couple of hard boiled eggs inside her meatloaf, but that's for another book.

Ingredients:
- 2 eggs
- ½ cup chili sauce
- 1 tablespoon soy sauce
- 1 tablespoon Worcestershire Sauce
- 1 teaspoon garlic powder
- ½ teaspoon powdered mustard
- ½ teaspoon pepper or to taste
- ½ cup bread crumbs
- 1 ½ lbs. lean ground beef
- 1 ½ lbs. lean ground turkey

Glaze
Mix together
- ¼ cup catsup
- ¼ cup brown sugar

Heat oven to 400° F.

Beat eggs in large bowl. Add chili sauce, soy, Worcestershire Sauce and all spices. Add bread crumbs. Add meat. Gently mix the meat with your hands until well blended. Put meat mixture into baking dish and mold into the shape of a half football. WASH YOUR HANDS. Pour glaze over the top and bake, UNCOVERED, for 1 hour.

HINT: Put foil on the bottom of the pan to make clean-up easier.

MY MOM'S MEATBALLS WITH CABBAGE
Prep Time: 15 minutes
Serves: a whole gaggle of people.

My mom sent me this (hence the title...duh). Not in an email attachment. Not via link to a food website. No, she sent it on a 3X5 card, handwritten, the way God intended recipes to be shared. Where she got it I don't know.
So don't sue me if you published it a million years ago.

Ingredients:
- 2 lbs. lean ground beef (Here's another instance when you can use lean because we're adding enough other stuff) You could also use a bag of frozen pre-cooked meat balls if you're feeling especially lazy
- ½ teaspoon S
- ¼ teaspoon P
- 1 small head of green cabbage
- 2 14.5 ounce jars of "Ragu" sauce (or similar if you get my drift)
- 1 14.5 ounce can of jellied cranberry – the solid kind, not the kind with chunks.

(I know, this is where you're scratching your head and going "hmm?" in that sing-songy voice. Bear with me, it's a crowd pleaser)

Heat oven to 350º F. Season the ground beef with salt and pepper and roll into 1-inch balls. Place on cookie sheet and bake 30 minutes.

Hack cabbage into 1-inch pieces. Dump spaghetti sauce, jellied cranberry and cabbage into a BIG pot and bring to a boil. Lower heat to simmer, add meatballs and COVER. Cook on very low heat for 1 hour.

This can also be made in a Crock Pot. Just add everything, including the cooked meatballs, to a Crock Pot and cook on low for 6 hours.

POLISH SAUSAGE
Prep Time: 1 minute
Serves 2 to 4

This one's real easy. You might be tempted to make it four times a week. But don't. It is high in salt and additives like sodium nitrates. It is also fairly greasy and not really a diet food. But it's great if you've run out of ideas and want something quick and easy. And oh yeah, it tastes great. Especially with hash browns, hot mustard and a dark beer.

Ingredients:
• Polish Sausage (can be purchased at the supermarket under many brand names)

Cut the sausage into 2 big pieces and place in skillet on medium heat. Brown on all sides, turning often. Use the same philosophy as bacon. Be patient and cook evenly on all sides. Serve, eat, save the leftovers – they're great for sandwiches the next day.

POLISH SAUSAGE WITH CABBAGE AND POTATOES
Prep Time: 10 minutes
Serves 2 to 4

This is a good one-pot meal. A word on one-pot meals: they can be a cook's best friend. You've been spending the last few days planning and executing whole meals. You're ready for some down time. Just be sure to make a lot of noise banging around in the kitchen so she thinks you're really working hard. **Now is not the time to lose any ground in your quest for the love nest.**

Ingredients:
- ½ head of green cabbage cut into large pieces
- Polish sausage cut into 1-inch chunks
- 2 medium or 3 small red potatoes per person, cut in half
- ½ teaspoon salt
- ¼ teaspoon pepper

You'll need your steamer for this recipe.

Place cabbage on the bottom of the steamer. Add the potato and sausage. Season with salt and pepper. Place steamer in the pan with about 2-inches of water. Bring to a boil. Lower heat to simmer and steam everything for about 30 minutes. Make sure you don't run out of water. You can always add more.

Serve this with hearty rye bread, hot mustard and, you guessed it...a nice dark beer.

SHISH KABOBS
Prep Time: 10 minutes
Serves 2 to 4

When I was growing up, marinating meant dumping a bottle of Wishbone Italian dressing (pronounce Eye-talian) in a bowl and adding your meat or chicken. While this is still a pretty good quick-fix option, making a marinade is pretty simple. We'll be using a basic marinade for this recipe that gives it a Mediterranean feel.

Ingredients:
- 1 lb. sirloin steak cut into 2-inch pieces
- ½ onion, cut into 2-inch pieces
- 8 to 10 button mushrooms
- 2 zucchinis, sliced into 1-inch pieces.
- 1 red bell pepper, cut into 2-inch pieces

For the Marinade:
- 1 cup olive oil
- juice of two lemons (Don't use the bottled stuff, if you don't have lemons, use ½ cup of white wine instead)
- 4 cloves garlic, smashed
- 2 teaspoons dried or 2 tablespoons fresh oregano or rosemary
- ½ teaspoon salt
- ¼ teaspoon pepper

Mix marinade Ingredients together then divide into 2 bowls: in one bowl add the meat, in the other, add the veggies. Let everything hang out for an hour or so.

You'll be cooking this on the grill, so now would be a good time to discover you're out of charcoal and run to the store. And don't forget to pick up some beer while you're out.

When you get back, start the fire. Take your metal skewers (there really is no substitute, and no, you can't use a wire hanger for many, many reasons) and load up some skewers with the meat. Make sure the pieces don't touch.

Then load up some more skewers with the veggies, alternating types as you go along. (You'll be cooking the meat and the veggies separately because the meat takes longer.)

Put the meat on the fire and cook, turning often, until they're the way you like them. ½ way through add the veggies. DON'T WALK AWAY FROM THE GRILL. Stand there and take it like a man. Turn your food. Drink your beer. When everything is cooked like you like it...it's eat time.

FLANK STEAK
Prep Time: 5 minutes
Serves 4 to 8

There are two important things to learn about flank steak. One, it needs to be marinated for a long time. Like overnight. And secondly, it needs to be sliced against the grain on the bias. What does that mean? Look at the meat. Notice how the sinews of the muscle all go in one direction. When you cut across the sinews holding your knife at a 45 degree angle to the cutting board you are cutting against the grain and on the bias. Wow, you learn something new everyday in the kitchen. Be sure to pontificate these new bits of newly found knowledge to you wife to gain even more "I didn't know you were smart AND sexy!" points.

You can use the kabob marinade, or a bottle of Wishbone Italian (Eye-talian as they say here in the Upper Midwest) dressing or you can ... improvise. Calm down. Don't panic. You should be ready by now to improvise.

Ingredients:
- Flank Steak
- Marinade (Use above recipe, or...you guessed it, a bottle of "Eye-talian" dressing)

Place steak in plastic bag. Add marinade. Seal and refrigerate overnight. Why overnight this time? Because flank steak is very tough. If you don't marinate it for at least 8 hours you might as well be eating a shoe.

When you're ready, make the fire for the grill. (You should have some charcoal left over because you bought a whole bag when you made the Kabobs, remember?)

When the fire is hot, remove steak from the marinade and cook on the grill to desired doneness. 4 minutes a side will be medium-rare. Remove from the fire to a platter. Let it hang out on the platter while you gather the troops for dinner. Slice the steak as indicated above.

EASY MEAT SAUCE FOR SPAGHETTI
Prep Time: 10 minutes
Serves 2 to 4

I know I've been saying that food made from scratch is better-tasting and better for you. But this recipe is so simple and basic I can't leave it out.

Ingredients:
- 1 lb. lean ground beef or turkey
- ½ teaspoon garlic powder
- ½ teaspoon dried oregano
- ¼ teaspoon pepper
- 1 24 oz. jar of your favorite spaghetti sauce

Brown the beef, season with the garlic powder, oregano and pepper. Add most of the jar of spaghetti sauce. Cover and simmer for 15 minutes while you prepare the spaghetti. Note to self on making spaghetti sauce: since you'll be cleaning the kitchen, be careful not to splatter. This stuff seems to migrate to the walls, floor and stove top like mosquitoes to Minnesota.

Here are some variations:

BAKED ZITI
Prep Time: 2 minutes
Serves 2 to 4

Ingredients:
- 1 lb. box of ziti, cooked according to package instructions.
- 1 ½ cups of Easy Meat Sauce
- ½ cup of shredded mozzarella
- ¼ cup grated parmesan cheese

Add meat sauce to drained pasta along with the parmesan cheese. Transfer to baking dish. Spread mozzarella cheese on top. COVER and cook for 15 minutes in a 350° F. oven. Remove cover and continue cooking another 5 to 10 minutes, until bubbly.

The Easy Meat Sauce can also be used to top your favorite pizza crust. Just add cheese.

SLOPPY JOES
Prep Time: 5 minutes
Serves 4 to 6

This is my sister's recipe. I just called to remind her but she didn't remember. Poor thing.

Ingredients:
- 1 lb. lean ground beef or turkey
- ½ teaspoon garlic powder
- ¼ teaspoon onion powder
- ¼ teaspoon red chili flakes
- 1 can condensed tomato soup (One of the rare times I'll recommend using a commercial canned soup in a recipe, so sue me)
- 1 tablespoon Worcestershire Sauce
- 1 tablespoon soy sauce

Brown the meat. Add the garlic powder, onion powder, and chili flakes. Add the tomato soup, Worcestershire Sauce and soy sauce. Cover. Simmer on low for 15 or 20 minutes.

Some people like to add chopped green peppers and onions, but I like it pure. Just meat and sauce. Nothing between me and my meat and my bun.

POT ROAST
Prep Time: 15 minutes
Serves 6 to 8

Making pot roast this way is a two-stage process: stove top and oven. If you want an easy version, you can always just dump a bunch of Ingredients in a Crock Pot and walk away for 10 hours. The following recipe will have a richer, more robust flavor. It's totally appropriate for a dinner party, whereas the Crock Pot version is an everyday kind of deal.

Note: I suggest that you use a Dutch oven for this recipe. A Dutch oven is a heavy baking dish that can be covered and can handle the heat on the stove top, as well as the oven. I have a cast iron Dutch oven I swiped from my mom's kitchen. She'll never miss it, since she hasn't made pot roast like this since women wore aprons and men drank Gin martinis and smoked filter-less cigarettes. You can buy a good cast iron Dutch oven at the big sporting goods store next to the mall. And they're cheap.

Ingredients:
- 2 tablespoons olive oil
- 3 to 4 lb. boneless chuck roast or arm roast
- S and P
- 2 carrots, chopped
- 1 onion, chopped
- 1 stalk of celery, chopped
- 2 tablespoons flour
- 1 bay leaf
- 2 tablespoons tomato paste
- 2 cups beef broth
- 10 to 12 small new potatoes

Heat oven to 325° F.

On medium-high heat, add the olive oil to your Dutch oven. Salt and pepper the roast and add to the pot. Cook the heck out of it on one side until it pulls freely away from the pan and has a nice brown crust but is not burned. Turn and repeat. Remove the roast to a plate. **Lower heat to medium low.** Add the all of the chopped veggies (not the 'taters') to the pan along with the flour. Sauté until veggies are cooked through (about 5 minutes.) Add the bay leaf and mix in the tomato paste and the beef stock. Return the roast to the pan. COVER and put in the oven for 2 hours. After 2 hours remove from oven and add the potatoes, cover. Return to the oven for 1 more hour.

The roast should sort of fall apart when it's done. Remove roast and potatoes from the pan. Fish out the bay leaf and throw it away. If you want a thicker gravy, mix 1 tablespoon flour in 1/3 cup hot water and add to the gravy. Bring back to a boil on the stove, lower the heat and simmer, uncovered, for ten minutes or so. Taste the gravy and adjust salt and pepper to taste.

To strain or not to strain, that's the question. Well, if you REALLY want to wow your guests, strain the gravy through a fine strainer and put in a gravy boat for service. If it's a pretty rustic and rowdy crowd, what the heck, just serve the whole mess as it is. I'm a strainer kind of guy myself. That's what gives people the impression that I can actually cook. Hah!

PORK

Let's talk pork. The big time food experts and high-end restaurateurs will tell you that you don't have to cook pork all the way through like you used to. The days of food-born illness from undercooked pork are over, according to them. Well let me tell you, in my house at least, a piece of undercooked pork will sit on a plate uneaten until it starts to grow legs. And if ordered in a restaurant, you'd think it had legs by the speed with which it would be sent back to the kitchen. Where I grew up, pork was cooked for TWELVE HOURS.

The following recipes don't require 12 hours of cooking, but the cooking times will reflect a piece of pork that is cooked ALL THE WAY THROUGH.

PORK TENDERLOIN
Prep Time: 5 minutes
Serves 4 to 6

Ingredients:
- 1 whole pork tenderloin (They often come packaged in twos, either cook them both and freeze one for later, or cook one and freeze one to have later)
- 1/3 cup soy sauce
- ¼ cup rice wine vinegar (or white wine)
- 2 cloves garlic, chopped
- 1 tablespoon chopped fresh ginger
- 1 jalapeno pepper, chopped fine
- 1 tablespoon honey or sugar
- ¼ teaspoon pepper

Mix together all Ingredients, except pork, in large bowl. Add pork to the pool. Let this slt for at least an hour, or up to 4 hours in the fridge.

Remove tenderloin from the marinade and put on a grill over medium-high heat. Brown on all sides, about 3 to 4 minutes a side. Shut down the grill or lower the flame and let it hang out over indirect heat for another 20 minutes. It should read 160° F. when tested with a meat probe. Let it rest for 10 minutes. Cut into 1 ½ inch medallions (that's a fancy foodie word for "slices." Call them medallions, and it will impress your intended target.)

Serve with your favorite sauce. Peanut sauce is a real crowd pleaser. There are some good packaged ones out there, but here is a simple recipe for a homemade one:

PEANUT SAUCE
Prep Time: 10 minutes

Ingredients:
- 1 cup crunchy peanut butter
- ½ cup chicken stock or water
- ¼ cup soy sauce
- 1 tablespoon rice wine vinegar
- 1 tablespoon toasted sesame oil
- 1 clove garlic, very finely chopped
- 1 teaspoon finely chopped ginger
- ½ teaspoon red chili flakes

Heat all Ingredients in a sauce pan over medium heat until boiling. Reduce heat to low and cook for 5 minutes, whisking often. Serve warm.

EASY BBQ PULLED PORK
Prep Time: 2 minutes
Serves 6 to 8

You'll need a Crock Pot for this recipe. You can also do it in the oven on a super-low heat…like 225° F….for 8 hours if you want. This recipe is NOT a substitute for REAL BBQ pulled pork. For that you need a smoker and a dry rub and that's fodder for another book. But a respectable sandwich can be made from this pork, especially if you top the sandwich with your favorite cole slaw.

Ingredients:
- 3 to 4 lb. pork roast, shoulder or butt (Interestingly enough, a pork "butt" is not actually the butt, but the shoulder. Go figure. Just as well – I'm not sure anybody really wants to eat a pig's ass)
- 1 onion, sliced
- 1 bottle of your favorite BBQ Sauce

Put the sliced onions in the bottom of your crock pot. Add the pork roast. Pour enough BBQ sauce to make it about ½ way up the roast. Cover and cook on low for 10 hours. The roast should fall apart in the sauce when it's done and make a darn fine 'sammy.' This is great for a party because people can serve themselves right from the Crock Pot. Be sure to have plenty of buns on hand (no pun intended.)

SMOTHERED PORK CHOPS WITH ONIONS AND APPLES
Prep Time: 10 minutes
Serves 4 to 6

Ingredients:
- 4 8 oz. bone-in pork loin chops
- 1 to 2 tablespoons olive oil
- 2 green apples, peeled and thinly sliced
- 1 onion, thinly sliced
- ½ cup chicken stock
- 1/3 cup apple cider vinegar
- 2 tablespoons brown sugar
- S and P
- ¼ teaspoon dried sage (optional)

In a skillet, brown the chops on both sides over medium heat in 1 to 2 tablespoons of olive oil. Remove them to a plate. Add the apples and onions to the pan and sauté until almost cooked through (about 2 minutes.) Add the, chicken stock, vinegar, sugar, sage, if using, and salt and pepper. Return chops to pan, COVER, and simmer on LOW for 45 minutes or until the chops are cooked to an internal temperature of 160° F. Serve with mashed potatoes.

CHICKEN

There are a bazillion chicken recipes out there. I'm giving you three that are easy, basic and can easily be improvised upon.

ORANGE CHICKEN
Prep Time: 5 minutes
Serves 2 to 4

The name describes the preparation, not the color of the chicken. No one should eat an orange chicken. There's kind of an Asian thing going on here so serving it with rice is nice.

Ingredients:
- 1 package of chicken thighs, bone-in or boneless, and skinless. They usually come 6 to a package. (You can use any chicken pieces you like, I think it works best with thighs because of their uniform size and rich flavor. Boneless, skinless breasts tend to dry out, no matter how much goo you put on them)
- ½ cup orange marmalade (about ½ a small jar)
- ½ cup soy sauce
- 1 tablespoon of toasted sesame oil
- ½ teaspoon red chili flakes

Heat oven to 350° F. Mix together the orange marmalade, soy sauce, toasted sesame oil and the chili flakes. Put chicken in baking dish and cover with the orange mixture. Bake for 1 hour, turning the chicken a couple of times.

CHICKEN DRUMMIES
Prep Time: 2 Minutes
Serves 2 to 4

The drummie is the part of the wing that looks like a chicken leg. I started cooking them because my wife gets grossed out by chicken parts, and these are easy to eat with little fussing. You can use the whole wing for this recipe as well; just be a nice guy and separate the drummie from the wing for service.

Ingredients:
- 1 package drummies (about 12 to 14 in a package)
- 1 small bottle of "Eye-Talian" dressing

Heat oven to 400° F.

In a bowl, pour the dressing over the drummies and let marinate for at least 30 minutes,

1 to 2 hours is best in the fridge.

Place marinated chicken (with the marinade) in a baking dish. Bake, UNCOVERED, for 45 minutes, turning a few times during cooking.

BAKED CHICKEN
Prep Time: 2 minutes
Serves 4 to 6

Ingredients:
- 1 2 to 3 pound whole chicken, washed and dried, with the package containing the guts removed (Seriously, people leave the thing inside during cooking and it becomes a humiliating joke for years to come at family get-togethers. Admit it, we've all heard about someone who left the thing inside the Thanksgiving turkey)
- 1 tablespoon olive oil
- S and P

Heat oven to 425° F. Rub the chicken all over with the olive oil. Sprinkle inside and out with salt and freshly ground pepper. This is not time to use cheap pepper from the little red metal box in your spice rack.

Place the chicken, breast-side up, on a rack that's been placed on a foil-lined sheet pan (you'll thank me later when you don't have to scrub chicken goo that's been baked onto the pan.) Cook chicken in the oven for 15 minutes at 425° F. Lower the heat to 350° F. and cook for another hour and 15 minutes. Total cooking time is 1 1/2 hours. About halfway through the cooking time, tip the chicken up so that the juices evacuate to the foil-lined pan. This will help to give you a crisp bird inside and out.

This is the simplest recipe for baked chicken. There are variations you can try. Stuff the chicken with ½ an onion and ½ an orange, lemon or a few carrots and some chopped celery. Or try glazing the chicken with a combination of soy sauce and honey. Brush on in the final 15 minutes.

EASY CHICKEN POT PIE
Prep Time: 10 minutes
Serves 2 to 4

Here's an idea for leftover chicken. (Some people don't like leftover chicken. My nephew thinks it tastes like fish, but then again, he's a rocket scientist, so go figure. I think it's fine, especially in an easy chicken pot pie!)

There are easier ways to make pot pie, namely by using canned cream of mushroom soup for the sauce...but not in this book. Those recipes are saved for the Church/Synagogue Auxiliary circa 1965.

Ingredients:
- ½ onion, chopped
- 2 stalks of celery, chopped
- 1 carrot, chopped
- 2 tablespoons butter
- 2 cups of leftover chicken, cut in fork-friendly chunks
- 2 cups of white sauce or chicken gravy (see recipe on page 48)
- ½ cup frozen peas
- ½ teaspoon of poultry seasoning (optional)
- ½ teaspoon salt
- ¼ teaspoon pepper
- 1 tube of refrigerator biscuits

Heat oven to 350° F.

In a large sauce pan, cook the onion, celery and carrots in the butter until soft. Add the

chopped chicken, white sauce or chicken gravy, frozen peas, poultry seasoning, salt and pepper. Pour mixture into a baking dish and top with the biscuits, leaving some space between them.

Bake for 45 minutes or until the biscuits are browned and the chicken mixture is bubbly. If you have extra biscuits, bake them up according the package instructions then keep them in the fridge until they turn into little beige hockey pucks. Then throw them away like I do.

BAKED SESAME CHICKEN
Prep Time: 10 minutes
Serves 3

Ingredients:
- 3 boneless chicken breasts
- ¼ cup sherry
- 1 teaspoon toasted sesame oil
- ¾ cup sour cream
- 1 cup sesame crackers crushed (substitute regular saltines and 1 teaspoon of sesame seeds)

Heat oven to 400° F.

Combine the sherry and oil and brush onto the chicken. Add sour cream to both sides of the chicken. Roll the chicken in the cracker crumbs. Place on a cookie sheet sprayed with non-stick cooking spray. Bake 25 to 30 minutes.

THE MORNING FOOD GROUP

A word of advice on breakfast...don't cook it. Don't start a bad trend. But if you absolutely have to (birthdays, Mother's Day, Sunday brunch,) cook at your own risk. If you're too good at it though, it might spill over into the work week. This would be a disaster.

SCRAMBLED EGGS
Prep Time: 5 minutes
Serves 2

Ingredients:
- 2 tablespoons butter
- 4 eggs
- S and P

Melt 2 tablespoons butter on low heat (Don't burn the butter! If you do, start over – don't try to cover up your mistake. Burnt butter with eggs tastes...well, burnt. And don't worry, we all burn the butter once in a while, and that's not a euphemism)

Break eggs into bowl and mix well with fork. Add a few drops of water and a dash of salt and pepper.

Dump in the eggs. Cook over LOW HEAT stirring constantly with your wooden spoon. When the eggs are fluffy and to your likeness, you may add a handful of grated cheese and cover. This is what we call a "gourmet touch." You can leave them in the pan, covered, for a couple of minutes, while you butter the toast and pour the coffee. But remember, grumble a lot at this point. You don't want anyone to think you *like* doing breakfast.

OMELETS

Once you've mastered the scrambled egg you can move on to omelets. You can put anything in an omelet. I've been known to use last night's Sloppy Joes with cheese in Sunday's omelet. Hey, I'll try anything once.

CHEESE AND SAUTÉED ONION OMELET
Prep time: 5 minutes
Serves 1

Ingredients:
- 2 eggs
- 2 tablespoons butter
- ½ cup chopped onions
- ½ grated cheese
- S and P

Melt butter on low in skillet. Add onion and cook until clear and remove from pan.
(Add another tablespoon of butter if the pan looks dry.)

Add 2 eggs (see above for egg prep) slowly to pan. Let them cook for a couple of minutes until they start to bubble up. Do not stir them. Let them make a big pancake. Add the cheese and onion. Cover for a minute or so.

THE TRICKY PART: This next step separates the chefs from the schlocks, and the zeros from the heroes:

FOLDING THE OMELET:

Turn off heat. Very carefully take a spatula and run it around the edges of the pan to loosen the egg. Flip the spatula under ½ of the omelet and quickly fold over. Cover and let it sit on low while you get the plate ready. You will serve your wife first, before you make another omelet for yourself. If you've gotten lazy by then just pour yourself a bowl of cereal.

HINT: Use three instead of two eggs and when the omelet is done, carefully remove from pan onto cutting board, chop in half. Each person gets ½ an omelet. Twice as nice for ½ the price.

OTHER OMELET IDEAS

Dice some ham or leftover steak and sauté with the onion. Sautéed mushrooms or tomatoes are nice too, but they can make an omelet soupy. Soupy is bad. Experiment. Being a good cook means being flexible and creative.

THE MORNING FOOD GROUP

EASY EGG CASSEROLE (AKA TRAILER PARK STRATA)

I stole this easy recipe from a friend's mom one Sunday morning. I admit it, I'm not above "borrowing" a good recipe. It's simple to make, yet it's still kind of fancy.

If your friends have run out of excuses to avoid your cooking, this is a perfect dish to dispel all of their misgivings once and for all.

Prep Time: 10 minutes
Serves 4 to 6

Ingredients:
- 8 eggs
- 6 slices of white bread (this is the only time I'll recommend white bread for anything)
- 1 lb. of grated cheddar cheese
- ½ cup milk
- ½ teaspoon salt
- ¼ teaspoon pepper

Arrange bread on bottom of a buttered 9x13 baking dish. Mix eggs in bowl with the milk, salt and pepper. Pour eggs over bread. Add cheese on top. Cover and refrigerate overnight.

The next day, Heat your oven to 350° F. Please do not do this the night before. Bake, UNCOVERED, for 45 minutes, until cheese is brown and bubbly. Remove pan from oven and let cool for a few minutes before serving. This gives you time to plate some store-bought cinnamon rolls and pour the coffee.

MAKIN' BACON

Sounds silly, doesn't it? Well we've all watched mom cook bacon and it's not as easy as it looks. Unless, of course, you like either tooth-chipping or limp, impotent bacon.

Do not preheat your pan. Spread bacon evenly so that it covers the bottom of the pan and turn the fire on low. Check the bacon regularly, but do not turn up the heat. Be patient. This is a pork product and pork likes to be cooked low and slow. Turn the bacon when it starts to get brown.

When the bacon starts to shrink, you can add a few more slices to the pan. Be careful. These new slices will cook faster than the first ones...they are boiling in the other slices' grease. (Sounds great, huh?)

Take out the finished slices. They should be crunchy but not brown. Keep watching the bacon and remove and drain all done slices on paper towels.

Put any unused cooked bacon in a plastic bag in the freezer for use on salads, etc... at a later time. Bacon is full of fat and high in calories and good bacon is expensive. But holy pork bellies, does it taste great!

TOAST

Ingredients:
    Bread
    Toast bread in toaster. If I need to tell you more than that, you're in bad culinary shape, and what's more, you're never going to make it to the bedroom with the wife if
    you can't AT LEAST make toast.

MOM'S SPECIAL BUT REALLY SIMPLE BRUNCH BAGEL

You need: One bagel per person. Butter. Cream cheese. Jam.
Cut bagel in half. Butter each half and put under the broiler on high for about
3 minutes or until the butter is melted and turning brown. Schmeer with cream cheese and jam.

I am purposefully not including lox (smoked salmon) in the recipe. It is expensive, and it tastes like a mistake of nature. (My opinion, I know. But this is my book.)

LUNCH

What are you cooking lunch for? Call a friend. Go OUT TO LUNCH. Let somebody wait on you for a change. You have your hands full cooking dinner.

THE WET FOOD GROUP:
SAUCES AND GRAVIES

In the world of cooking to impress then undress, using sauces is like getting the keys to the city. It says "I love you more than just this dry ol' chicken and rice. I love you with this chicken and rice gently napped in rich gravy!"

WHITE SAUCE

The fancy word for this is Béchamel. Use it to impress or get laughed at, depending on your gene pool. White sauce is used in dishes that typically call for "Cream of ... Soup". This sauce is also used in a dish that brings back horrible childhood memories. Just writing it down gives me chills. It was called...Chipped Beef on Toast. Ahhhhh!!

Ingredients:
- 2 tablespoons butter
- 2 tablespoons flour
- 2 cups of milk, room temperature milk
- nutmeg
- Tabasco sauce
- S and P

Melt butter over low heat in a sauce pan. Whisk in the flour. Keep whisking over low heat until the flour starts to turn an off-white color, about 5 minutes. (This is called a roux and if it burns you'll be starting over. There's no saving a white sauce that starts with a burned roux.)

Next, slowly pour in the milk, whisking all the while. Cook this mixture over low heat until it starts to get thick (about 5 minutes.) It can come to a gentle boil. Add ¼ teaspoon of nutmeg, couple dashes of hot sauce and S and P to taste. (Some people say to use white pepper so there aren't black flecks in the sauce. If little black flecks in your white sauce bother you that much, then be my guest.)

BEEF/CHICKEN GRAVY

Brown is typically used with meat and potato combinations – Meatloaf and mashed potatoes, pot roast and red potatoes. You get the idea.

For beef gravy, replace the milk in the above White Sauce recipe with beef stock.

Use ½ chicken stock and ½ milk and you have chicken gravy. Use pork stock and you have pork gravy. Use turkey stock and you have turkey gravy. Use ½ beef and ½ chicken and you have "mock veal." (Mock like "fake" not mock like what your teenager does to you when you wear an Aerosmith Tee shirt.)

All of these stocks can be found in the grocery store packaged either in cans or boxes. Some companies make concentrated stocks, but they tend to be very salty and contain mystery Ingredients that have names too long to pronounce. I'm just sayin,' the better the stock, the better the sauce or gravy.

MUSHROOM GRAVY

Prep Time: 15 minutes

Mushroom gravy can be used the same way as brown gravy with meats

Ingredients:
- 8 oz. button mushrooms, sliced
- 2 cups brown gravy
- 1 clove garlic, chopped
- 2 tablespoons butter
- S and P

In a skillet over medium-high heat, melt butter and add mushrooms and garlic. Cook mushrooms until soft. Season to taste with salt and pepper. Whisk into the brown gravy and heat through.

Makes 2 Cups

WINE SAUCE (WHITE)

OK, if you haven't been able to tell by now, I'm not a classically trained chef. I've probably made every mistake in the book. But I *have* been cooking for people a long time. I know what works and what doesn't ... and I know my limitations. This wine sauce is simple. That's why I make it. It has a clean taste that works well on fish, chicken or pasta.

Ingredients:
- 1 tablespoon olive oil
- 2 tablespoons chopped shallots
- 1 cup good, dry white wine
- 2 tablespoons butter
- Juice of ½ a lemon
- S and P

Sauté the shallots in olive oil over medium-low heat. Add the wine and reduce on low heat by ½. ("Reduce" means that you start with 1 amount and cook it slowly until it ends up half as much, hence it "reduces" by ½.) Add the lemon juice, salt and pepper to taste. Whisk in the butter to finish sauce. Now is a good time to throw in some chopped, fresh herbs (parsley, thyme, basil) if you have them. But you don't have to.

WINE SAUCE (RED)

Ingredients:
- 1 tablespoon olive oil
- 1 tablespoon minced shallots
- ½ cup red wine
- ½ cup beef stock
- 1 tablespoon Dijon mustard
- ½ teaspoon dried thyme, or a couple of sprigs of fresh thyme
- S and P to taste

Sauté the shallots in the olive oil until clear but not browned. Add the wine and stock and reduce by ½ on medium-low heat. Whisk in the Dijon. Add in the thyme and salt and pepper to taste. This sauce is good with red meats like beef or lamb.

THROWING A DINNER PARTY

You've learned your lessons well. You've impressed the heck out of your better half, and now it's time to bring in the 'hood. Your first dinner party will be for a manageable four people with leftovers. I'll give you a sample menu, some timelines and a few tips along the way.

I have a few "rules to live by" when it comes to throwing a dinner party.

Rule Number One: ALWAYS have some food ready when your guests walk in the door. If you're anything like me, when I get invited out (which is rare) and I have the prospect of free food staring me in the face, I'm going to starve for most of the day to get ready. So when I walk into my hosts' house and there is NOTHING to munch on and dinner is 20 minutes away, I start getting weak in the knees and my vision gets fuzzy around the edges. And take it from me, a beer does not an appetizer make. A couple of "beer appetizers" and you're really going to be weak in the knees. It doesn't have to be fancy – just some cheese and crackers or nuts. Pita and hummus is nice with some good Greek olives.

Rule Number Two: Turn off the TV. Unless everyone is there to watch "the big game," nobody wants to hear monster truck ads during cocktail hour.

Rule Number Three: Don't clean the kitchen when your guests are still in your home. Dumping out smelly leftovers and stacking plates or loading them into the dishwasher is fine, but leave the kitchen clean-up for later. It makes people feel like you're hustling them out when you start cleaning right away. And whatever you do, DON'T accept help from your guests to clean the kitchen. They didn't come to your house to clean. Although it does sound interesting to throw a house cleaning party...

THE MENU
Starters:

Pita bread cut into triangles, store-bought hummus (put it in a bowl and no one will know) and some Greek olives. Be sure to put an empty bowl by the olives for the pits or they may end up stuffed between the seat cushions.

The Main Course:
Green Salad with Honey Mustard Vinaigrette
Pot Roast with New Potatoes

Dessert:
Nothing *you've* got to worry about. When your guests ask you what they can bring, always tell them dessert. Even if they just bring a carton of ice cream it's still better than having to make something yourself.

THE SCHEDULE

You've told your company to be there at 6:00 pm. With some people that means 6:30 and with others it means 5:45. Be ready if they come a knockin' fifteen minutes early. And you're making pot roast because it holds in case they're late.

12:00 Start cleaning the house. This is best done by delegation. Delegate the house cleaning to the wife. Tell her you're in charge of the kitchen. If she knows she won't have to clean the kitchen, she'll probably be OK with swabbing down the terlits.

3:00 Prep Ingredients for the pot roast

3:30 Start cooking the pot roast. You want it done by 6:30 and it will hold for 30 minutes

4:45 Set the table

5:00 Set up the bar. Depending on your tastes, this could be nothing more than bottled water and ice for glasses. If not, then this is the time to open the red wine. Make sure the white is chilling. The beer is cold. The ice bucket is filled. And the appropriate glasses are out for whatever people are drinking. In addition to adult beverages, always make sure there are plenty of non-alcoholic choices available, both diet and non-diet.

5:30 Cut pita bread in quarters and arrange on a platter around the olives and the hummus.

6:00 Guests arrive. While your partner gets their drinks, you start tearing the lettuce for the salad and making the dressing. They will be SO impressed when they see all of the fresh Ingredients come together for the vinaigrette. Such a pro you are!

6:30 Remove pot roast and potatoes from the pan. Slice or let the pot roast fall apart on the serving tray. Arrange the potatoes around. Skim as much visible fat as possible from the gravy. Pour the remaining gravy (strained or unstrained...see recipe) in a bowl or gravy boat.

6:45 Add dressing to the salad and toss. Don't toss the salad one minute sooner than you need to or it will be a soggy mess.

Dinner is served!

So now chef, you've done it! You've planned, shopped and prepared an awesome meal for your wife and friends. Dinner has been enjoyed, the wine is flowing and the clock is ticking. Your wife has been "smiling" at you all night. Letting little naughty jokes seep into the conversation with a wink and a nudge to you. It's time for the gentle reminder to your friends that "Oh boy, (yawn) it's getting kind of late." (Most people get the hint. But obviously not my wife and me. We had a friend who would stand up, say good night and retire to his bedroom, leaving us all sitting mid-sentence at the table. We've since learned to pack it in at the first yawn.)

So the company's gone and you say to your wife, "Why don't you relax for while, dear? You've worked hard cleaning the house today. Get your jammies on and watch some TV in bed. I'll get the kitchen organized." Finally, all of your hard work is going to pay-off. It's booty time! Your mind is reeling from all of the things you're going to try. There's a movie playing in your head and it ain't rated PG. You've never cleaned the kitchen, brushed your teeth, combed the one hair you have left, and slapped on a little "Ode d 'Joy" with more speed. Up the stairs, two at a time. Open the door to heaven and there's your little angel in bed. Snoring like a lumberjack with her mouth hanging open and a little dribble of spit finding its way onto the pillow. Disappointment doesn't begin to cover it. But now SHE OWES YOU. **BIG TIME**.

SOME MENU IDEAS
Sizzlin' Sunday

(Use the leftover steak for sandwiches or a salad topper. Remember to make extra baked potatoes to have leftovers for home fries)

- Flank Steak
- Baked Potatoes
- Sautéed Spinach

MEATLESS MONDAY
- Baked Mac and Cheese
- Salad

TEMPTED NOT TO COOK TUESDAY
- Polish Sausage with Cabbage and Potatoes
- Salad

HAVE A NICE HUMP DAY
(You'll be using a lower oven temp for the chicken than the veggies, but it will still work fine and you can make them both in the oven at the same time on 350° F.)

- Orange Chicken
- Roasted Veggies
- Rice

THRILLED TO BE THURSDAY
- Meatloaf
- Mashed Potatoes and Mushroom Gravy
- Roasted Cauliflower

FRICKEN' FINGER LICKEN FRIDAY ALREADY
(SAVE THE LEFTOVER CHICKEN FOR THE POT PIE)
- Baked Chicken
- Southwestern Corn Pudding
- Salad

SO NOT HAPPY TO BE COOKING ON SATURDAY
- Sloppy Joes
- Home Fries
- Salad

WHAT!? IT'S SUNDAY AGAIN?
- Chicken Pot Pie (You have the leftover chicken, right?)
- Braised Brussels Sprouts

MONDAY MONDAY
- Pork Tenderloin
- Mixed Veggies "Chinese" Style
- Rice

GOTTA COOK ON TUESDAY
- Baked Ziti
- Salad

SHEESH WEDNESDAY'S HERE
- Shish Kabobs
- Rice
- Steamed Veggies

TOTALLY NOT COOKING THURSDAY
- Time to Order a Pizza

STEAK HOUSE FRIDAY
(Ok, I know you didn't cook last night, but after all the effort that will go into this meal getting lucky is a given)

- Steak Andrew Ellis
- Baked Potatoes
- Creamed Spinach

SATURDAY SURPRISE

- Peanut Butter
- 4 Slices White Bread
- Chips
- 16 beers

OTHER COMBINATIONS WITHOUT THE CUTE WEEKDAY NAMES:

- Polish Sausage, Home Fries and Baked Beans
- Meatloaf, Caramelized Sweet Potatoes with Pecans, Steamed Veggies
- Sloppy Joes, Baked Beans, Salad
- Chicken Drummies, Mixed Veggies "Chinese" Style
- Pork Tenderloin with Peanut Sauce, Asian Cole Slaw, Rice

Made in the USA
Charleston, SC
19 November 2009